CHALLE   FALSE LOGIC PUZZLES

Norman D. Willis

Sterling Publishing Co., Inc.
New York

Books by Norman D. Willis
Amazing Logic Puzzles (1994)
Tricky Logic Puzzles (1995)
False Logic Puzzles (1997)
Challenging False Logic Puzzles (1997)

Edited by Claire Bazinet

Library of Congress Cataloging-in-Publication Data Available

10 9 8 7 6 5 4 3 2 1

Published by Sterling Publishing Company, Inc.
387 Park Avenue South, New York, N.Y. 10016
© 1997 by Norman D. Willis
Distributed in Canada by Sterling Publishing
c/o Canadian Manda Group, One Atlantic Avenue, Suite 105
Toronto, Ontario, Canada M6K 3E7
Distributed in Great Britain and Europe by Cassell PLC
Wellington House, 125 Strand, London WC2R 0BB, England
Distributed in Australia by Capricorn Link (Australia) Pty Ltd.
P.O. Box 6651, Baulkham Hills, Business Centre, NSW 2153, Australia
Manufactured in the United States of America

Sterling ISBN 0-8069-9720-6

CONTENTS

Before You Begin

Solving logic puzzles is an active way of developing your thinking power. The puzzles in this book are all of a formal logic nature, requiring that you think a problem through and reason deductively in arriving at the solution. Each section in this book contains a different type of logic puzzle, and each presents a different kind of challenge. They do, however, share one thing: they all contain false statements which must be identified before you can achieve the correct solutions.

Use trial and error as a method in solving these logic puzzles. The information provided in each will afford a number of alternatives. Assume each in turn leads to the correct solution, and look for contradictions. When you have discarded unsatisfactory assumptions, what remains is the solution.

Diagrams are of value to aid in organizing and analyzing your assumptions. Suggested diagrams to use are provided in both the Hints and Solutions sections.

Whether or not you are new to logic puzzle solving, you will find many in this book that challenge your reasoning ability. As you gain experience solving them, you will find yourself meeting the challenge of more difficult puzzles— and you will enjoy the satisfaction that comes from successfully arriving at the correct solutions.

The puzzles range widely in degree of difficulty. Each section begins with the least difficult of a given type of puzzle and progresses to the most difficult. They are graded from one to three asterisks, as follows:

*	Challenging
**	Tantalizing
***	Mind Expanding

If you need assistance solving any particular puzzle or type of puzzle, the Hints section will be helpful. Considerations in solving each puzzle can be found in the Solutions section. For each puzzle, these describe an appropriate method to use to arrive at the solution. These will help you in solving other puzzles of the same type.

However, do not turn to the answer until you are sure you have given it your best effort.

Norman D. Willis

— 1 —

The Road Signs of Lidd

Visitors to the kingdom of Lidd are informed that they will be safe only as long as they follow the right roads, since dragons wait for the unwary who stray. There are, however, a significant number of crossroads and other road divisions and, since there were previously no road signs, many a visitor took a wrong turn and met with misfortune.

To correct the problem, the court magician was ordered by the king to place directional signs at all road divisions. With a wave of his wand he accomplished the task. Perhaps his powers were not strong enough. At any rate, it was found that many of the signs were false. In fact, in every grouping of road signs, one or more were false.

Visitors were assured that, with careful analysis, the road signs could be correctly and conclusively interpreted. However, they were cautioned that at each division of roads there was only one safe choice; the others would invariably cause a traveler to meet with disaster.

P1-1 The First Road Division*

One confident visitor who has important business in the kingdom proceeds along a main road. In time he arrives at a fork in the road, and reads two signs, one at each alternative road, as follows:

A
> This is the road to take unless it is B.

B
> A dragon waits along road A.

The traveler is reminded that at each road division there is at least one false sign. Which road should be taken?

(Hint on page 46)

(Solution on page 56)

P1-2 The Second Road Division*

The visitor makes the right decision. Before long, he is faced with another choice of roads. His three options are as follows:

A
> Signs B and C are true.

B
> Road A is the one to take, or else C is the correct road.

C
> Road B is not the one to take.

Which road should be taken?

(Hint on page 46)

(Solution on page 56)

P1-3 The Third Road Division*

The visitor, still proceeding on the safe road and still confident, approaches still another crossroad. He is presented with these three choices:

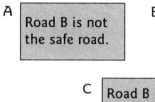

A · Road B is not the safe road.

B · Do not take this road.

C · Road B leads to a dragon.

Which is the right road to take?

(Hint on page 46)
(Solution on pages 56–57)

P1-4 The Fourth Road Division*

The visitor, having made the correct decision, continues on his journey. He soon arrives at a crossroad, with signs indicating a choice of three directions. The three signs are:

A · You should not come this way.

B · This is the road to take, or else C is the right road.

C · There is a dragon waiting near road A.

Which road is the safe one?

(Hint on page 46)
(Solution on page 57)

9

1-5 The Fifth Road Division*

Still continuing along the correct road, the visitor soon comes upon another three-way branching of the road. He considers the following signs:

A
At least one
of signs B and
C is true.

B
At least one of
signs A and B
is true.

C
Don't take road C.

Which is the correct road to take?

(Hint on page 46)
(Solution on page 57)

P1-6 The Sixth Road Division*

Still proceeding on the safe road, the visitor arrives at another road division. He consults these signs:

A
At least one of roads B
and C leads to a dragon.

B
Road B is the safe road, or
else A is the road to take.

C
At least one of roads A
and B leads to a dragon.

Which is the road to take?

(Hint on page 46)
(Solution on pages 57–58)

P1-7 The Seventh Road Division*

The visitor, still on the right road, approaches another crossroad. He considers the three road signs:

A
Both this road and road C lead to dragons, unless road B leads to a dragon.

B
Road A does not lead to a dragon, unless road C does not lead to a dragon.

C
Both road A and road B lead to dragons, unless this road leads to a dragon.

Which road should the visitor take?

(Hint on page 46)
(Solution on page 58)

P1-8 The Eighth Road Division*

Still on the right road, but proceeding less jauntily, the visitor comes to another division. This time there are four options, as follows:

A
Both roads B and C lead to dragons, unless road D does.

B
The sign at road C is true, unless A is the correct road to take.

C	Both roads B and D lead to dragons, unless this road does.	D	The sign at road A is true, unless road A is the one to take.

The confused and frustrated visitor flips a coin and proceeds along one of the four roads. No one ever sees or hears from him again. Which road should have been taken?

(Hint on page 46)
(Solution on pages 58–59)

— 2 —

More Dragons of Lidd

Dragons are on the endangered species list in the kingdom of Lidd. To protect them the king has decreed that knights may no longer slay dragons that refrain from devouring farm animals or their owners. The dragons that are cooperating with the decree are known as rationals. Some dragons, however, continue their traditional carnivorous ways in spite of the decree. They are known as predators.

Dragons in Lidd also vary by color and veracity. Gray rational dragons always tell the truth, and red rational dragons always lie. Red predator dragons always tell the truth, and gray predator dragons always lie.

Although it would be helpful to know a dragon's color, humans in Lidd are subject to an endemic affliction: they are all color-blind. To each knight, all dragons look gray, which makes it more puzzling to determine which dragons it is acceptable to slay.

Your challenge is to identify the color and type of each dragon encountered in these puzzles.

P2-1 What Color?*

Two knights encounter a dragon, who quickly responds, "I am protected by the king's decree." Gray rational dragons and red predator dragons always tell the truth; red rational dragons and gray predator dragons always lie.
    What color is he?

(Hint on page 46)
(Solution on page 59)

P2-2 What Type?*

A knight encounters a dragon and asks if he is one of the protected ones. The dragon answers "I am red."
    Is he a rational dragon or a predator dragon?

(Hint on page 46)
(Solution on page 59)

P2-3 An Outnumbered Dragon*

Two knights in armor approach a lone dragon, who quickly makes the following statements:

Dragon
    1. I am not a predator.
    2. I am either red or gray.

What is he?

(Hint on page 46)
(Solution on page 59)

P2-4 Who Are Protected?*

Two dragons are approached by two knights, who inquire as to the color and type of each. They answer, as follows:

A. 1. B and I are protected by the king's decree.
   2. B and I are both red.

B. 1. A's statements are false.
   2. I am gray.

What color and type are the two dragons?

(Hint on page 47)
(Solution on page 60)

P2-5 Three Dragons*

Three knights confront three dragons, who make the following statements:

A. 1. C is not a gray rational.
   2. I am a predator.

B. 1. I am not a gray rational.
   2. A is red.

C. 1. I am a rational.
   2. B's statements are false.

What color and type is each of the three dragons?

(Hint on page 47)
(Solution on page 60–61)

P2-6 Three More Dragons*

Three knights on the lookout for an adversary confront three dragons, who offer these statements:

A. 1. I am a rational.
   2. B's statements are false.

B. 1. C is a rational.
   2. I am a predator.

C. 1. A's statements are false.
   2. B is a gray predator.

What are the color and type of each dragon?

(Hint on page 47)
(Solution on page 61)

P2-7 An Outnumbered Knight**

A knight in armor searching for a dragon not protected by the king's decree encounters three dragons. He asks each about his color and type. They respond, as follows:

A. 1. I am definitely a rational.
   2. Either B or C is a rational.
   3. Neither B nor I am red.

B. 1. I am not one of the protected dragons.
   2. A is gray.

C. 1. I am protected.
   2. A is red.
   3. B is a gray predator.

What are each dragon's color and type?

(Hints on page 47)
(Solution on page 62)

P2-8 An Outnumbered Knight Again**

A knight on horseback rounds a corner and confronts three dragons. In response to the knight's inquiry, they speak as follows:

A. 1. B and I are not the same type.
   2. I am red.

3. C and I are not the same color.

B. 1. C and I are not the same color.
2. A's statements are true.

C. 1. A and I are not the same type.
2. B and I are the same color.

What are the color and type of each dragon?

(Hint on page 47)
(Solution on pages 62–63)

P2-9 Surrounded by Dragons***

A knight on horseback, negotiating mountainous terrain, finds himself surrounded by four fierce dragons. Maintaining a bold manner, he demands that each dragon state his color and type. Their responses follow, although D remains silent:

A. 1. D would claim that B's statements are false.
2. B is red.
3. C and D are different colors.

B. 1. A would claim that C's statements are true.
2. D is red.
3. A and I are the same color.

C. 1. All four of us are predators.
2. D and I are red.
3. A and B are gray.

D.

What are the color and type of each of the four dragons?

(Hint on page 47)
(Solution on pages 63–64)

— 3 —

The Cases of
Inspector Detweiler

There are some within Inspector Detweiler's shire who do not always obey the laws. This extraordinary sleuth has been faced with several crimes that require solving. Your challenge is to determine which suspects are telling the truth and which are not, and who are the guilty.

P3-1 Who Stole the Stradivarius?*

A famous violinist was in town for a concert. While he was away from his room for a short time his favorite violin, a Stradivarius, was stolen. The inspector took immediate action, and through diligent research was able to identify four suspects. Each of them makes one statement as follows. The guilty one's statement is false; the other statements are true.

A. I was not in town at the the time of the theft.
B. C is the culprit.
C. B's statement is false.
D. C's statement is true.

Which one is guilty?

(Hints on page 48)
(Solution on pages 64–65)

P3-2 The Forest Robber*

A notorious robber has made a lucrative living by robbing travelers in the forest. Inspector Detweiler has, after extensive examination of the available clues, identified three suspects. Their statements follow. One makes two true statements; one makes one true and one false statement; one makes two false statements.

A. 1. I am not the robber.
   2. C is the robber.

B. 1. C is innocent.
   2. A is the robber.

C. 1. I am not the robber.
   2. B is innocent.

Which one is the robber?

(Hints on page 48)

(Solution on page 65)

P3-3 Two Pickpockets*

Two pickpockets were plying their trade at the village fair. The inspector's review of the clues indicated that there were two culprits working together. He has interrogated four suspects who are known pickpockets. The two who are guilty each make only one true statement. Little is known as to the truthfulness of the statements made by the other two suspects. Determine the two who are guilty from their statements below:

A. 1. B is one of the culprits.
   2. C would never be guilty of such a crime.
   3. D is a disreputable character and certainly could be one of the culprits.

B. 1. A's first statement is true.
   2. C is one of the culprits.
   3. If C is not one of the culprits, then either A or D is guilty.

C. 1. A's second statement is true.
   2. B is not one of the guilty ones.
   3. B's second statement is true.

D. 1. A's third statement is true.
   2. B's second statement is true.
   3. C's second statement is false.

(Hints on page 48)
(Solution on pages 65–66)

P3-4 The Poacher*

A closed hunting season in the forest has been declared. Hunting has been considered a source of food for some, and, consequently, poaching has become a problem. Inspector Detweiler has been requested to bring to a halt a series of illegal appropriations of game. Clues indicate that there is one culprit, and the inspector has identified four suspects. The four make statements below. The truthfulness of their statements is unknown, except that only one of the guilty suspect's statements is true.

A. 1. D is innocent.
   2. I am not the poacher.
   3. Hunting is a source of food in these parts.

B. 1. C's being a suspect is a case of mistaken identity.
   2. A's second statement is true.
   3. Not all of my statements are true.

C. 1. I am not the poacher.
   2. D is the poacher.
   3. My being a suspect is not a case of mistaken identity.

D. 1. A's statements are not all true.
   2. At least one of C's statements is true.
   3. I do not like to eat game.

Which one is the poacher?

(Hints on page 48)
(Solution on page 66)

P3-5 Property Destruction at the Village Inn*

Five local villagers were having a late evening political discussion at the village gathering place. As the night wore on, the discussion deteriorated into a debate and then into an excessively noisy argument.

At this point, the proprietor attempted to intervene in order to quiet the disturbance. In the ensuing fracas, an expensive candelabrum was knocked over and broken. The five customers immediately vacated the premises.

Inspector Detweiler recorded the statements below in attempting to determine who broke the candelabrum. Not all of the statements are truthful. In fact, only one suspect makes no false statements.

Butcher
   1. I was not even there.
   2. The cobbler was looking for trouble; he did it.
   3. The candlestick maker helped him do it.

Baker
   1. I agree with the butcher's first statement.

2. The candlestick maker did not do it.
3. I agree with the butcher's second statement.

Candlestick Maker
   1. I did not do it.
   2. The butcher was there.
   3. The baker did it.
   4. The cobbler did not do it.

Blacksmith
   1. If the proprietor had not intervened this would not have happened.
   2. None of us is to blame.
   3. The candlestick maker is innocent.
   4. The cobbler did not do it.

Cobbler
   1. I agree with the baker's third statement.
   2. The candlestick maker did it.
   3. I was not looking for trouble; I did not do it.
   4. The baker did not do it.

Which one is guilty?

(Hint on page 48)

(Solution on page 67)

P3-6 Two Are Guilty**

In a series of thefts, it was found that there were two culprits working together. The inspector was able to identify five suspects, and the five each make two statements, below. One of the thieves makes two true statements. The other guilty one makes two false statements. Little is known as to the truthfulness of the statements made by the three innocent suspects.

A. 1. I was nowhere near the scene of the crime that day.
   2. B is innocent.

B. 1. I am innocent.
   2. E's first statement is false.

C. 1. I have no idea who the guilty ones are.
   2. D's statements are both false.

D. 1. C's second statement is not true.
   2. A is not guilty.

E. 1. A and B are the thieves.
   2. At least one of D's statements is true.

Which two are guilty?

(Hints on page 48)
(Solution on page 68)

P3-7 Pickpocket Thefts**

A notorious pickpocket had evaded apprehension for some time. The inspector redoubled his efforts to bring him to justice, and his keen detection work resulted in four suspects, all of whom were in town during the last known theft. One of them is guilty. Each makes three statements. If either A or C is guilty, each of the four suspects makes two true statements and one false statement. If either B or D is guilty, no two of the four suspects make the same number of true statements.

A. 1. I was out of town during the last known theft.
   2. Neither D nor I did it.
   3. C did not do it.

B. 1. A was in town during the last known theft.
   2. I am innocent.
   3. D is the guilty one.

C. 1. A is the pickpocket.
   2. B's first statement is false.
   3. B's third statement is false.

D. 1. The pickpocket deserves to be apprehended.
   2. At least one of B's statements is false.
   3. A is not guilty.

Who is guilty?

(Hints on page 48)
(Solution on page 69)

P3-8 D Is Missing**

A professional burglar has recently managed to actively pursue his criminal activities by targeting the homes of the most affluent villagers. The inspector is on the trail of the culprit and has identified four suspects, one of whom is missing. The other three are questioned; each makes two true statements and one false statement.

A. 1. I am not the burglar.
   2. D has no alibi.
   3. D went into hiding.

B. 1. A's first statement is true.
   2. A's third statement is false.
   3. D is not the burglar.

C. 1. I am not the burglar.
   2. D has an alibi.
   3. B's second statement is false.

Who is the burglar?

(Hints on pages 48–49)
(Solution on page 70)

P3-9 The Unlucky Car Thief**

A car thief who had managed to evade the authorities in the past unknowingly took the automobile that belonged to Inspector Detweiler. The sleuth wasted no time and spared no effort in discovering and carefully examining the available clues. He was able to identify four suspects, with certainty that one of them was the culprit.

The four make the statements below. In total, six statements are true and six are false.

A. 1. C and I had met many times before today.
   2. B is guilty.
   3. The car thief did not know it was the inspector's car.

B. 1. D did not do it.
   2. D's third statement is false.
   3. I am innocent.

C. 1. I had never met A before today.
   2. B is not guilty.
   3. D knows how to drive.

D. 1. B's first statement is false.
   2. I do not know how to drive.
   3. A did it.

Which one is the car thief?

(Hints on pages 49)
(Solution on pages 70–71)

P3-10 The Oldest or the Youngest***

A thief has been taking sheep from farmyards in the area, and there are four suspects. The inspector has been able to determine that the guilty one is either the oldest or the youngest of the four. They make the following statements, although each suspect makes only one true statement.

A. 1. B is the oldest among us.
   2. The youngest among us is guilty.
   3. C is innocent.

B. 1. A is not the youngest.
   2. D is the guilty one.
   3. D is the youngest.

C. 1. A is the youngest of the four of us.
   2. I am the oldest.
   3. D did not do it.

D. 1. The oldest among us is innocent.
   2. B is guilty.
   3. I am the youngest.

Which one is guilty?

(Hints on page 49)
(Solution on pages 71–72)

— 4 —

The Outliers of Hyperborea

According to the ancient Greeks, Hyperborea was a land to the north of Mount Olympus, home of the gods. The inhabitants were favored by the gods; they lived for a thousand years in a land of perpetual springtime, and they were free from pestilence.

Little known were the Hyperboreans' unique standards of veracity. Those who lived in the southern region of the land were known as Sororeans and they always spoke truthfully; those who lived in the northern region were known as Nororeans and they always spoke falsely; those who lived in the middle region were known as Midroreans and they made statements that were alternately truthful and false, but in which order was unknown.

There were a few rebels, called Outliers, who disdained the normal conventions of Hyperborea and refused to adhere to the accepted standards of veracity. Their statement patterns as to truth and falsehood were anything that was different from other inhabitants (that is, if three or more statements were made, there were some true statements and some false statements, but not in an alternating pattern).

P4-1 Whose Group?*

Hyperboreans belong to three groups: Sororeans, Nororeans, and Midroreans. Of the three inhabitants who make the statements below, little is known as to their group or groups except that Outliers are not present.

A. 1. B and I are both Midroreans.
   2. C is a Nororean.

B. 1. A and I belong to two different groups.
   2. C and I belong to the same group.

C. 1. I am not a Nororean.
   2. A and I belong to the same group.

To what group or groups do A, B, and C belong?

(Hints on pages 49–50)
(Solution on pages 72–73)

P4-2 An Outlier**

Four Hyperboreans are engaged in conversation. One is a Sororean, one is a Nororean and one is a Midrorean. The fourth speaker is an Outlier.

From their statements below, which one is the Sororean, which one is the Nororean, which one is the Midrorean, and which one is the Outlier?

A. 1. I am the Outlier.
   2. D is the Nororean.

B. A's first statement is true.

C. 1. I am not the Outlier.
   2. B is not the Midrorean.

D. C's first statement is true.

(Hints on page 50)
(Solution on pages 73–74)

P4-3 One of Each**

Among four Hyperboreans one is a Sororean, one is a Nororean, one is a Midrorean and one is an Outlier. They make the following statements:

A. 1. I am the Outlier.
   2. D is not more truthful than I am.
   3. B is the Sororean.

B. 1. A is the Outlier.
   2. C is not the Sororean.
   3. I am not the Midrorean.

C. 1. A is not the Outlier.
   2. B is not the Sororean.
   3. I am more truthful than D is.

D. 1. B is not the Nororean.
   2. A's second statement is false.
   3. C's third statement is false.

Which one is the Sororean, which one is the Nororean, which one is the Midrorean, and which one is the Outlier?

(Hint on page 50)
(Solution on pages 74–75)

P4-4 Olympic Games**

It is not commonly known that the original Olympic Games occurred not in Olympia, Greece, but in Hyperborea. Three Hyperborean Olympic athletes are discussing the results of the recent competition. Inhabitants of Hyperborea belong to three groups: Sororeans, Nororeans and Midroreans. There are also those few Outliers.

Their groups are unknown except that exactly one of the athletes is an Outlier.

A. 1. I was the winner of the one-half league run.
   2. You can count on what C says to be truthful.
   3. I am not a Midrorean.

B. 1. A did not win the one-half league run.
   2. I entered three events.
   3. C is the Outlier.

C. 1. I am not the Outlier.
   2. B's second statement is truthful.
   3. A did not win the one-half league run.

What are the groups of the three athletes?

(Hints on page 50)
(Solution on page 76)

P4-5 One Is an Outlier**

Outliers, although few in number, occasionally make their presence known. Hyperboreans are either Sororeans, Nororeans, Midroreans, or those few Outliers. As to the four inhabitants who make statements below, little is known as to their standards of veracity, except that exactly one of them is an Outlier.

A. 1. B is the Outlier.
   2. D is a Sororean.
   3. C is a Midrorean.

B. 1. I am not the Outlier.
   2. A is a Nororean.

3. C is not a Midrorean.

C. 1. I am not a Midrorean.
  2. B is not the Outlier.
  3. D is a Sororean.

D. 1. I am a Sororean.
  2. B is the Outlier.
  3. A is a Midrorean.

To which group does each of the four Hyperboreans belong?

(Hint on page 50)
(Solution on pages 76–77)

P4-6 Olive Picking**

Olives are an important staple in Hyperborea, and olive picking is an occupation engaged in by many inhabitants. Four olive pickers are having a discussion. One is known to be a Sororean, one is known to be a Nororean, one is known to be a Midrorean, and one is known to be an Outlier. Their statements follow:

A. 1. I picked more olives today than anyone else.
  2. I am the Midrorean.
  3. C is the Outlier.

B. 1. I am the Midrorean.
  2. I would have picked more olives today than A, except that I did not start until after lunch.
  3. C is the Outlier.

C. 1. D dropped more olives than he picked.
  2. I picked more olives today than A did.
  3. B picked olives all day today.

D. 1. C picked more olives today than A did.
   2. I did not drop any olives today.
   3. B would have picked more olives than A today, except that he did not start until after lunch.

Which one is the Sororean, which one is the Nororean, which one is the Midrorean, and which one is the Outlier?

(Hint on page 50)
(Solution on pages 77–78)

P4-7 Four for the Races***

Four Hyperboreans are practicing for the upcoming chariot races. They are known to be a Sororean, a Nororean, a Midrorean, and an Outlier. They make the following statements:

A. 1. This race track is slow.
   2. D is doing so well in practice that he will win.
   3. C is the Outlier.

B. 1. A's first statement is true.
   2. I am the Midrorean.
   3. D is the Nororean.

C. 1. This race track is fast.
   2. I agree with B's second statement.
   3. I am not the Nororean.

D. 1. I am doing so poorly in practice that I will lose.
   2. B' second statement is false.
   3. A is the Sororean.

Which one is the Sororean, which one is the Nororean, which one is the Midrorean, and which one is the Outlier?

(Hint on page 50)
(Solution on pages 78–80)

P4-8 Six Hyperboreans***

Six Hyperboreans hold the jobs of chariot maker, fishnet weaver, musician, olive grower, tax collector, and wine maker. One is known to be a Sororean; two are known to be Nororeans; two are known to be Midroreans; one is known to be an Outlier. They make statements as follows:

Agenor
1. As olive grower I have the most important job.
2. Cadmus is the chariot maker.
3. Philemon's third statement is true.

Alphenor
1. Philemon is not the fishnet weaver.
2. I find my work as tax collector to be very satisfying.
3. Now that Hesperus is the chariot maker, we have been winning more races.

Cadmus
1. Agenor claims to be the olive grower, but that is my job.
2. Alphenor is the tax collector.
3. Hesperus is the chariot maker.
4. Everything that Philemon says is false.

Callisto
1. The last tour I took with my lyre was so successful I intend to schedule another one.
2. Everything that Agenor says is true.
3. Cadmus is not the chariot maker.

Hesperus
1. We have been winning very few chariot races lately.
2. Agenor is the wine maker.

3. Cadmus is the tax collector.
4. I am the fishnet weaver.

Philemon
1. I am the tax collector.
2. Callisto is the musician.
3. Hesperus's statements are all true.
4. Cadmus is the olive grower.

Which Hyperborean is the Sororean, which are the Nororeans, which are the Midroreans, which is the Outlier, and what is the job of each?

(Hints on page 50)

(Solution on pages 80–82)

P4-9 Chariot Race Winners***

The winners of chariot races were among the heroes of the Hyperboreans. Five such honored ones were discussing the number of chariot races they had won. Each has had more than three wins; no two have had the same number of wins; and each chariot racer's number of wins is divisible by three. The one with the most wins is the Grand Champion. Of the five chariot race winners, little is known except that exactly one of them is an Outlier.

From their statements below, what is the standard of veracity of each, how many chariot races did each win, and which one was the Grand Champion?

Agathon
1. Lysis is the Grand Champion.
2. Protagoras has had 15 wins.
3. Lysis is a Sororean.
4. Phaedrus is not the Outlier.

Lysis
1. Sosias is the Outlier.
2. Phaedrus is a Sororean.
3. I am not the Grand Champion.
4. Agathon is not the Grand Champion.

Phaedrus
1. I have had 18 wins.
2. Agathon is the Grand Champion.
3. Lysis is the third highest in the number of wins.
4. Protagoras is the Outlier.

Protagoras
1. Agathon has had fewer wins than Lysis.
2. Sosias has had 15 wins.
3. Lysis is the Outlier.
4. Agathon has had more wins than I have had.

Sosias
1. I have had more than six wins.
2. Agathon has had more wins than Protagoras.
3. Phaedrus is the Outlier.
4. Phaedrus's third statement is false.

(Hints on page 50)
(Solution on pages 82–84)

— 5 —
Fragments

Among those who particularly enjoy logic puzzles, some prefer more than any other the type of puzzle that contains several statements, each one of which provides a fragment, or a limited amount, of pertinent information. In total, the statements afford enough, but just enough, to enable the solution to be found.

The puzzles in this section represent several of this type, with one exception: each puzzle contains a false statement, which must be identified before you can arrive at the correct solution.

As in all logic puzzles, men have male-sounding names and women have female-sounding names. There will never be, say, a man named Barbara or a woman named Bob.

P5-1 The Midville Muddlers*

The Midville Muddlers baseball team depends on four players to score most of their runs. The positions of the four are the three outfielders (right fielder, center fielder, and left fielder) and the catcher. From the statements that follow, determine the first name (Henry, Ken, Leo, or Stan), surname (one is Dodson), position, and batting average of each player. (Their batting averages are .280, .295, .310, and .325.) One of the following statements is false.

1. Neither Leo nor the catcher has a batting average over .300.
2. Three who are neighbors are Clements, the right fielder, and the player who bats .325.
3. The center fielder bats .295.
4. Stan's batting average is 30 points higher than that of Ken, who does not live near any of the other three.
5. Brooks and Henry, who is not Ashley, both bat over .300 and are in competition to see which will score the most runs this season.
6. Henry, who is neither the right fielder nor the left fielder, has a lower batting average than the catcher.

(Hints on page 51)
(Solution on pages 84–85)

P5-2 Fishing Vacation Plans*

Carl and three of his friends who are avid fishermen decided to visit four of the world's finest sport fishing locations over a period of four years. Each friend had a different favorite location, so they chose the order in which they would take the trips by drawing the place names from a hat. Based on the statements below, what is the first name (Andy, Bill, Carl, or Dennis) and surname (one is Cole) of each friend, what was the favorite fishing location of each, and what was the order in which the trips were to be taken? One of the statements below is false.

1. Andy and Barrott work for the same company; Bill is self-employed.
2. The Iceland trip was planned for the year before the Alaska trip, which was not Andy's favorite destination.
3. Carl and Barrott and their wives frequently play bridge together.
4. Whelan's favorite fishing location was the third trip,

which was neither Patagonia nor New Zealand.
5. Whelan and Cole are married; the other two are not.
6. Dennis was disappointed that his favorite destination, New Zealand, was not to be the first; Crowley's favorite destination was planned for the last trip, so he was unsympathetic.
7. Barrott's favorite destination was the first.

(Hints on page 51)
(Solution on pages 85–86)

P5-3 White-Water Rafting*

Eight friends decided to try white-water rafting on a nearby river. They rented four two-person rafts; one was yellow, one was green, one was red, and one was blue. They selected partners for the four rafts and agreed on a destination at the end of a white-water run. Based on the following statements, one of which is false, what is the first name (Alan, Don, Frank, Henry, LeRoy, Paul, Phil, or Walt) and surname (Cook, Gladstone, Hawley, Hughes, O'Brien, Sands, Smith, or Wilson) of each of the friends; which were partners on the four rafts; and what color raft was used by each?

1. Phil and Cook, who were in the same raft, arrived at the destination without incident, but they were not the ones who finished first.
2. The red raft capsized and did not finish; the green raft was first to finish the white-water run.
3. O'Brien and LeRoy were not on the same raft.
4. Paul and Wilson finished last on their raft.
5. Fortunately, Henry is a good swimmer, and he helped his partner, Hughes (whose first name is not Walt), get to shore. They were able to recover their capsized raft, but declined to finish the white-water run.
6. Frank was the first to select a raft, and he picked the

yellow one. He and Hawley were on the second raft to finish the white-water run.

7. Alan and Hughes were on the same raft; they were the first to finish the white-water run.

8. LeRoy and Smith completed the run and were not in last place.

9. After their nearly tragic capsizing experience, Don and his partner, Gladstone, vowed not to set foot in another raft.

10. Alan did not care that he and his partner finished last; he was just glad that they made it.

(Hints on page 52)
(Solution on pages 86–87)

P5-4 Spelling Contest**

There were five finalists in the city schools spelling contest this year. They competed until four of the five misspelled a word, and the fifth one was declared the winner. From the following statements, one of which is false, what is the first name and surname (Jennings, Knudson, North, Olsen, or Salisbury) of each finalist; who missed what word; and what was the order in which they finished the competition?

1. North, who was not the one who misspelled "physiognomy," had not participated in a spelling contest before. He said he had not expected to do well.

2. "Vicissitude" was misspelled immediately after "bivouac" and immediately before "isthmus."

3. Eleanor was happy that her good friend Jennings was one of the two finalists in the contest.

4. Before Eric misspelled his word there were only two contestants left; he and Olsen had studied together in preparation for the contest.

5. Gordie, who lasted longer in the competition than Jennings, was not the winner.
6. Knudson, who is not Helen, was the first to misspell a word.
7. Helen, Jennings, and Olsen are neighbors.
8. Jennings told Lois that she could not sleep the night before the contest.

(Hints on page 52)
(Solution on page 87)

P5-5 Audubon Field Trip**

Four married couples, who are members of the Audubon Society, undertook a bird-watching field trip to identify the varieties of birds to be observed in the local woods. To cover a sufficient area, each couple walked in a different direction. It was agreed that, for birds that were not common in the region, any sightings were to be recorded as to the time of the sighting and the name of the first person to see and identify the bird. At the end of the day, it was found that a different person was the first to sight each of eight uncommon birds.

From the following statements determine the first name and surname (Brinkley, Dwyer, Eng, or Valentine) of each member, and the variety of bird observed by each. One of the following statements is false.

1. Neither James, Curtis, Mr. Brinkley, nor either of the Valentines was the first to sight a western tanager.
2. William was the first to sight a golden-crowned kinglet; he and his wife live near the Brinkleys.
3. Both Rosemary and Nancy, neither of whom is Valentine or Dwyer, were attending their first Audubon meeting and field trip, although both their spouses have been active members for several years.

4. Nancy was the second to sight a western tanager.
5. As program chairperson, Curtis's spouse is quite active active in the local Audubon Society chapter and arranges and attends all their outings.
6. A lazuli bunting was first sighted by Angela, who only attends an occasional Audubon Society chapter meeting or outing.
7. Nancy was disappointed that her husband, Curtis, sighted an acorn woodpecker before she sighted her bird.
8. A pine siskin, which was sighted early in the day, and a yellow warbler were first sighted by Mr. and Mrs. Dwyer, not necessarily in that order.
9. Harold was first to sight a white-crowned sparrow, at about the same time that Nancy sighted her bird in a different part of the woods; her bird was not a black-headed grosbeak.
10. Curtis was the last to sight his bird.

(Hints on page 53)
(Solution on pages 88–89)

P5-6 Car Pool**

Six business people travel to and from work in a car pool van driven by a seventh person. The six are picked up each workday morning where they live and are returned home each evening. From the statements that follow, for each of the business people determine the first name (one is Milton), surname (one is Altchech), occupation (one is a computer programmer), sequence of pickup in the morning, and sequence of drop-off in the evening. (Due to traffic patterns, the evening drop-off sequence is not necessarily the reverse of the morning pickup sequence.) One of the statements is false.

1. Amarol feels that she is fortunate to be the first one dropped off in the evening.
2. Neither Neal, Florence, Agassi, nor Atwater is the secretary.
3. Paul is the sixth to be picked up in the morning, but Avenal is the first to be dropped off in the evening.
4. The word processing supervisor is the third to be dropped off in the evening; the secretary is the second to be picked up in the morning and the fifth to be dropped off in the evening.
5. Adams, the attorney, dislikes having to be the first to be picked up in the morning and the last to be dropped off in the evening.
6. Gloria is picked up in the morning immediately after Neal and immediately before Paul. In the evening she is dropped off immediately after Avenal and immediately before Amarol, who is dropped off immediately before Evelyn.
7. Avenal, who is not the systems analyst, and Amarol are members of a men's choral group.
8. The personnel manager, who is not Atwater, is not the fourth or fifth to be picked up in the morning.

(Hints on page 53)
(Solution on pages 89–90)

P5-7   Summer Students***

Six students at the university decided to each take one class during the summer session. Each selected a separate subject conducted by a different professor. On the campus there are six buildings in a row, identified consecutively as A to F. Each student attended class in a different one of the six buildings.

Identify each student's first name and surname (Karr, Peterson, Rogers, Sawyer, West, or Williams), class subject (one is economics), professor, and the building in which the class attended was held.

1. Louise, whose surname is not Karr, and Rogers attend classes in adjacent buildings; neither of them is studying English.
2. Carl, who is studying history, attends class in a building that is adjacent to both Sawyer's and Burt's building.
3. Victoria's classroom building is next to that of Peterson.
4. Professor Denton, whose subject is not music, does not teach in a building adjacent to that of Professor Carson.
5. Professors Harrison and White teach in buildings that are at the two ends of the row; neither teaches psychology or music.
6. Building B—which is neither the music building nor the building in which Williams attends his class—is where Professor Landers teaches.
7. Professor Carson's building is not D; his law students this summer are all men.
8. John takes law from Professor White two buildings from where Professor Harrison teaches.
9. Neither Fran, Williams, nor Peterson have their class in a building at either end of the row.
10. Rogers feels fortunate to have Professor Landers as an instructor; John feels the same way about his professor, whose building is next to that of Professor Harrison.
11. Sawyer is one of Professor Bradford's best students.

(Hints on page 54)
(Solution on pages 91–93)

P5-8 Chess Players***

Each of six members of the City Chess Club has his or her preferred series of opening moves and no two prefer the same opening. Three of the preferred openings are king's pawn openings and three are queen's pawn openings. The three king's pawn openings are the Bishop's Opening, the King's Gambit, and the Ruy Lopez. The three queen's pawn openings are the Stonewall System, the Colle System and the Queen's Gambit. Each player also has a preferred defense against king's pawn openings and a preferred defense against queen's pawn openings. No two prefer the same defense.

From the following statements, one of which is false, determine each member's first name (Dan, Edith, Fred, George, Harry, or Jeff), surname (one is Davis), preferred opening, and preferred defense (one defense against queen's pawn openings is the Benoni Defense).

1. George and Gruber are two of four members who are evenly matched and enjoy competing against each other; the other two are the one who prefers the King's Gambit opening and the one who prefers the Sicilian Defense against king's pawn openings and the Tarrasch Defense against queen's pawn openings.
2. Draper always opens with the Stonewall System when he has the white pieces; he dislikes the French Defense against king's pawn openings, and rarely uses the Cambridge Springs Defense against queen's pawn openings.
3. Duvall and Fred, neither of whom uses the French Defense or the Caro-Kann Defense against king's pawn openings, usually win when they play any of the other four.
4. The one who prefers the Bishop's Opening prefers the Pirc Defense against king's pawn openings and the

Meran Defense against queen's pawn openings, except when playing Harry, who is by far the strongest player among the six members.

5. Campbell, whose first name is not Edith, likes the King's Gambit because of the number of possible variations; Jeff prefers the Ruy Lopez.
6. Edith always opens with a king's pawn.
7. The second-strongest player is Evans, who does not open his games with the Queen's Gambit; when defending against queen's pawn openings, he does not use the Nimzo-Indian Defense.
8. The player who prefers to open with the Colle System does not use Petroff's Defense when defending against king's pawn openings.
9. The player who usually opens with the Stonewall System believes that it gives her the best chance to be competitive.
10. The player who favors the Two Knights Defense against king's pawn openings does not use the Cambridge Springs Defense against queen's pawn openings; one of the players who favors a king's pawn opening favors the King's Indian Defense against queen's pawn openings.

(Hints on page 55)
(Solution on pages 93–95)

HINTS

H1 THE ROAD SIGNS OF LIDD

For these puzzles, it was given that there is at least one false sign in each group of signs. Therefore, each puzzle can be solved by determining which sign or signs are false. However, be sure that your decision is conclusive.

H1-1 The First Road Division Is sign A true or false?

H1-2 The Second Road Division Could sign A be true?

Considering puzzles **1-3** to **1-7**, prepare a diagram, such as the following, and indicate T or F, assuming each road in turn to be the correct one:

	sign A	sign B	sign C
if road A			
if road B			
if road C			

H1-3 The Third Road Division Could A be the safe road?

H1-4 The Fourth Road Division Could B be the safe road?

H1-5 The Fifth Road Division Is sign C true or false?

H1-6 The Sixth Road Division Is sign A true or false?

H1-7 The Seventh Road Division Could road A be the safe road? If not, why not?

H1-8 The Eighth Road Division Which sign or signs are false?

H2 MORE DRAGONS OF LIDD

H2-1 What Color? If the dragon has made a false statement, or told the truth, what color is he?

H2-2 What Type? If the dragon has made a false statement, or told the truth, what type is he?

H2-3 An Outnumbered Dragon What can you conclude from the dragon's second statement?

For puzzles **2-4** to **2-9**, construct a diagram with color and type on one axis and each speaker listed on the other axis, as illustrated below.

	A	B	C
Color			
Type			

As you draw conclusions, indicate red or gray and rational or predator in the diagram.

H2-4 Who Are Protected? From A's two statements, could he be telling the truth?

H2-5 Three Dragons Consider B's first statement. What conclusion can you draw?

H2-6 Three More Dragons Consider C's second statement and B's second statement. Could C's statement be true?

H2-7 An Outnumbered Knight If A's statements are true, what color and type is he? Is this consistent with the statements by B and C?

H2-8 An Outnumbered Knight Again Assume B's statements are true. Are they consistent with the statements by A and C?

H2-9 Surrounded by Dragons Consider C's statements. Are they consistent with those of the other dragons?

H3 THE CASES OF INSPECTOR DETWEILER

For puzzles **3-1** to **3-9**, construct diagrams listing the suspects on one axis and the statement numbers on the other. The example below will illustrate:

	I	2	3
A			
B			
C			

Indicate T or F as you form conclusions about each suspect's statements. Assume that each suspect, in turn, is guilty; test each assumption against the truthfulness of all statements.

H3-1 Who Stole the Stradivarius? Consider that the guilty suspect's statement is false; the other statements are true. Assume that each suspect in turn is guilty. In each case, is this consistent with the statements by the other suspects?

H3-2 The Forest Robber Consider that one suspect makes two true statements, one makes one true statement and one false statement, and one makes two false statements. Assume that A is guilty. What can you conclude about the statements of B and C?

H3-3 Two Pickpockets Consider that the two who are guilty each make only one true statement. Assume that B is guilty; does this assumption hold up?

H3-4 The Poacher Consider that only one of the statements made by the guilty is true. Assume that B is guilty; test B's three statements against this assumption.

H3-5 Property Destruction at the Village Inn Consider that only one suspect makes all true statements. Can you locate that suspect?

H3-6 Two Are Guilty Consider that one of the two culprits makes two true statements; the other makes two false statements. Assume that A is guilty. Test this assumption against the statements made by the other four suspects.

H3-7 Pickpocket Thefts Consider that if A or C is guilty, each suspect makes two true statements. If either B or D is guilty no two suspects make the same number of true statements. As you assume each in turn to be guilty, carefully assess the statements of the four suspects against these guidelines.

H3-8 D Is Missing Consider that each suspect makes two true and one false statement. Assume that C's second statement is his false one. Test this assumption against the statements by all three.

H3-9 The Unlucky Car Thief Consider that there are six false statements. What can you tell from A's first statement and C's first statement, and from C's third statement and D's second statement?

H3-10 The Oldest or the Youngest A diagram, such as below, is suggested.

	I	2	3	oldest	youngest
A					
B					
C					
D					

Consider that the guilty one is either the oldest or the youngest, and that each suspect makes only one true statement. Assume that A's first statement is true. Is this consistent with his second and third statements?

H4 THE OUTLIERS OF HYPERBOREA

For each of these puzzles construct a diagram such as the one below and indicate plus or minus as you draw conclusions regarding each speaker:

	Sororean	Nororean	Midrorean	Outlier
A				
B				
C				
D				

H4-1 Whose Group? If you assume that A's first statement is true, what does this tell you about B's first and second statements? Also, what does this imply about C's statements?

H4-2 An Outlier This puzzle (as well as the puzzles that follow) includes an Outlier, whose standard of veracity is different than those of other Hyperboreans. To be different, an Outlier must make two consecutive statements that are truthful and one that is false, not necessarily in that order; or two consecutive statements that are false and one that is true, not necessarily in that order.

We know that all four types are represented. If you assume that A's first statement is true, his second statement could be true or false. What are the possibilities for B, C, and D?

H4-3 One of Each If A's first statement is true, what would that tell you about his third statement?

H4-4 Olympic Games If you assume that A's first statement is true, what could you say about his third statement, and what conclusion could you draw about A's type? If so, what could you say about A's second statement?

H4-5 One Is an Outlier If you assume that B is the Outlier, what can you say about B's third statement?

H4-6 Olive Picking What can you conclude from A's second statement and B's first statement?

H4-7 Four for the Races Assume that A's third statement is truthful. If so, what does that tell you about A's type?

H4-8 Six Hyperboreans We know that there are one Sororean, two Nororeans two Midroreans, and one Outlier among the six speakers. Philemon's first and third statements are contradictory. What does that tell you about Philemon? (This does not necessarily make him the Outlier.) What other inconsistencies can you discover among the speakers?

H4-9 Chariot Race Winners If you assume that Agathon's third statement is truthful, what would that tell you about Agathon? How about Lysis?

H5 FRAGMENTS

For each puzzle in this section, assume that the statements are true until you encounter a contradiction. Then analyze those statements that involve the contradiction and other closely related statements until you can isolate the false one.

H5-1 The Midville Muddlers Set up a diagram to aid in organizing your conclusions. Below is a suggested diagram:

first name	surname	position	batting avg.

Since there are two players who bat below .300, statements 1 and 3 indicate that Leo must be the center fielder. However, from statement 6, Henry must be the center fielder. One of these three statements must be the false one.

H5-2 Fishing Vacation Plans A diagram such as the following will be helpful:

first name	surname	favorite location	order of trips

Statements 1, 3, 6, and 7 indicate that Barrott's first name is not one of the four individuals. One of these four statements must be false.

H5-3 White-Water Rafting The diagram below will be helpful in organizing your conclusions:

first name	surname	raft color

Statement 5 tells us that Henry and Hughes were on the same raft. Statement 7 indicates that Alan and Hughes occupied the same raft. One of these two statements is false.

H5-4 Spelling Contest A diagram such as below is suggested to aid in organizing your conclusions:

first name	surname	word misspelled	place

Among the five contestants, three are young ladies. Statements 7 and 8 indicate that Jennings, one of the three, is not Lois or Helen. From this we can conclude that Jennings is Eleanor. This conclusion, however, is contradicted by statement 3. One of these three statements is false.

H5-5 Audubon Field Trip The diagram following will be helpful to you:

first name	surname	bird sighted

From statements 3 and 5, Curtis's spouse is not Nancy. However, statement 7 contradicts this. One of these three statements is false.

H5-6 Car Pool Set up a diagram such as below:

first name	surname	occupation	AM pickup	PM drop-off

Of the six business people, three are women. From statement 1, Amarol must be one of the three women. This, however, is inconsistent with statement 7. One of these two statements is false.

H5-7 Summer Students The diagrams below will be helpful to you:

first name	surname	subject	professor	building
Burt				
Carl				
Fran				
John				
Louise				
Victoria				

professor	subject	building
Bradford		
Carson		
Denton		
Harrison		
Landers		
White		

Statement 5 indicates that Professors Harrison and White teach in buildings at opposite ends of the row. This is contradictory with statement 8. One of these two statements is false.

H5-8 Chess Players Set up a diagram to help you, such as the one following:

first name	surname	preferred opening move	preferred king's pawn defense	preferred queen's pawn defense

Of the six members of the club, Edith is the lone female. From statement 9, she usually opens with the Stonewall System. However, from statement 6, she prefers a king's pawn opening. The Stonewall System is a queen's pawn opening. Therefore, one of these two statements is false.

SOLUTIONS

S1-1 The First Road Division

CONSIDERATIONS
The sign at road A is true, since it covers both roads. Therefore, the sign at road B must be false. Road A is the correct road.

SUMMARY SOLUTION Road A is the one to take.

S1-2 The Second Road Division

CONSIDERATIONS
The sign at road A must be false, as it was given that at every road division at least one sign was false. Therefore, either the sign at road B or the sign at road C is false, or both are false.

   If road A is the right choice, the signs at roads B and C are both true, which presents a contradiction. If road C is the correct choice, again the signs at roads B and C are both true. Therefore, the correct road must be B.

SUMMARY SOLUTION Road B is the right road to take.

S1-3 The Third Road Division

CONSIDERATIONS
All three signs agree that B is not the road to take. Therefore, since at least one sign is false, they are all false. The correct road must be B.

	sign A	sign B	sign C
if road A	T	T	T
if road B	F	F	F
if road C	T	T	T

SUMMARY SOLUTION Road B is the correct road to take.

S1-4 The Fourth Road Division

CONSIDERATIONS

If road B is the correct choice, all three signs are true. If road C is the correct choice, again all three signs are true. If road A is correct, all three signs are false. Therefore, road A is the one to take.

	sign A	sign B	sign C
if road A	F	F	F
if road B	T	T	T
if road C	T	T	T

SUMMARY SOLUTION Road A is the correct choice.

S1-5 The Fifth Road Division

CONSIDERATIONS

If C is not the road to take, then sign C is true. That would mean that sign A is true, so sign B would also be true. But all three signs can't be true, so C is the road to take.

	sign A	sign B	sign C
if road A	T	T	T
if road B	T	T	T
if road C	T/F	T/F	F

SUMMARY SOLUTION C is the safe road.

S1-6 The Sixth Road Division

CONSIDERATIONS

The signs at roads A and C must be true, since there is only one safe road. Therefore, B is the false one; neither A nor B is safe. Road C is the road to take.

	sign A	sign B	sign C
if road A	T	T	T
if road B	T	T	T
if road C	T	F	T

SUMMARY SOLUTION Road C is the correct one.

S1-7 The Seventh Road Division

CONSIDERATIONS
If road A is the correct choice, all three signs are true. If road C is the correct choice, all three signs are true. Therefore, road B is the correct choice. The signs at roads A and C are true; the sign at road B is false.

	sign A	sign B	sign C
if road A	T	T	T
if road B	T	F	T
if road C	T	T	T

SUMMARY SOLUTION Road B is the correct choice.

S1-8 The Eighth Road Division

CONSIDERATIONS
If the safe road is either B, C, or D, all four signs are true. Therefore, since at least one sign is false, A is the road to take. The implication in sign A is that if road D leads to a dragon, at least one of roads B and C is safe. The implication in sign C is that if road C leads to a dragon, at least one of roads B and D is safe. Only the signs at roads B and D are true.

	sign A	sign B	sign C	sign D
if road A	F	T	F	T
if road B	T	T	T	T
if road C	T	T	T	T
if road D	T	T	T	T

SUMMARY SOLUTION Road A is the one the visitor should have taken.

S2-1 What Color?

CONSIDERATIONS

If the dragon is telling the truth, he is a gray rational; if he is lying, he is a gray predator.

SUMMARY SOLUTION The dragon is gray.

S2-2 What Type?

CONSIDERATIONS

If the statement is true, he is a red predator dragon, since a red rational would lie. If the statement is false, he is a gray predator, since a gray rational would tell the truth.

SUMMARY SOLUTION He is a predator dragon.

S2-3 An Outnumbered Dragon

CONSIDERATIONS

From the dragon's second statement, which covers both colors, we can conclude that he is telling the truth. From his first statement, the dragon must be a gray rational.

SUMMARY SOLUTION He is a gray rational.

S2-4 Who Are Protected?

CONSIDERATIONS

If A's first statement is true, A and B are both rationals. However, rational dragons that speak the truth are gray. Therefore, since A's second statement claims he is red, A's statements must be false. At least one of the two dragons is not a rational, and at least one of the two dragons is gray.

From B's first statement, we can conclude that B speaks the truth; and from B's second statement, B is a gray rational. Therefore, A must be a gray predator.

	A	B
color	gray	gray
type	predator	rational

SUMMARY SOLUTION

A. gray predator
B. gray rational

S2-5 Three Dragons

CONSIDERATIONS

B's first statement must be true. It would be a lie for a gray rational, and gray rationals always tell the truth. B must be a red predator.

Assume that A's statements are false. If so, from B's second statement, which is true, A is a red rational. If so, since A claims that C is not a gray rational, C must be a gray rational. However, C's second statement is false, since we know B's statements to be true.

Therefore, A, whose statements are true, is a red predator, and C, whose first statement is false, must be a gray predator.

	A	B	C
color	red	red	gray
type	predator	predator	predator

SUMMARY SOLUTION

A. red predator
B. red predator
C. gray predator

S2-6 Three More Dragons

CONSIDERATIONS

Assume that C's statements are true. If so, A's and B's statements are both false. However, B's second statement indicates that B is a predator, which agrees with C's second statement as to type.

Therefore, C's statements must be false. A's statements must be true. A is a gray rational. B, whose statements are false as indicated by A, must be a red rational. From B's first statement, C must be a gray predator.

	A	B	C
color	gray	red	gray
type	rational	rational	predator

SUMMARY SOLUTION

A. gray rational
B. red rational
C. gray predator

S2-7 An Outnumbered Knight

CONSIDERATIONS

Assume A's statements are true. If so, he is a gray rational. If so, C's statements must be false, as his second statement asserts that A is red. If so, from his first statement C is a predator and, from A's second statement, B must be a rational, whose first statement is false. However, his second statement affirms that A is gray, which would be the truth, an inconsistency.

Therefore, A's statements must be false. Therefore, A is a gray predator, and B, whose statements are true, is a red predator. From C's statements, which are false, we can conclude that C must be a gray predator.

	A	B	C
color	gray	red	gray
type	predator	predator	predator

SUMMARY SOLUTION

A. gray predator
B. red predator
C. gray predator

The knight quickly left the area.

S2-8 An Outnumbered Knight Again

CONSIDERATIONS

Assume B's statements are true. If so, from B's second statement, A's statements are also true. If so, from A's second statement, A must be a red predator, and from A's first statement, B must be a gray rational. If so, from B's first statement and C's second statement, which are contradictory, C must have lied. If so, C must be a red rational.

However, from C's first statement, C and A must be the same type, which is a contradiction.

Therefore, B's statements are false, as are A's. A, who claims to be red, is a gray predator, and from A's first statement, B is also a gray predator. C, whose second statement contradicts B's first statement, has spoken truthfully. C is a gray rational.

	A	B	C
color	gray	gray	gray
type	predator	predator	rational

SUMMARY SOLUTION

A. gray predator
B. gray predator
C. gray rational

S2-9 Surrounded by Dragons

CONSIDERATIONS

Assume that C's statements are true. If so, C and D are red predators, and A and B are gray predators. If so, however, B's second statement that D is red would be true, an impossible statement for a gray predator.

Therefore, C's statements are false. At least one of the four dragons is a rational; at least one of C and D is gray; and at least one of A and B is red.

Assume that B's statements are true. If so, according to B's first statement, A would claim that C's statements are true. However, since we know that C's statements are false, if B's statements are true, A's statements must be false. If so, from A's third statement, C and D must both be the same color, and from C's false second statement, that color must be gray. However, B's second statement indicates that D is red, which could not be the case. Therefore, B's statements must be false, and, from B's second statement, D is gray.

From B's first statement, which is false, A would claim that C's statements are false, which we know to be the case. Therefore, A's statements are true. From A's second statement B must be a red rational. From A's first statement D would claim that B's statements are false, which we know to be the case. Therefore, D is a gray rational. From A's third statement, C and D are different colors. Therefore, C is a red rational. From B's third false statement, A must be a gray rational.

	A	B	C	D
color	gray	red	red	gray
type	rational	rational	rational	rational

SUMMARY SOLUTION

A. gray rational
B. red rational
C. red rational
D. gray rational

S3-1 Who Stole the Stradivarius?

CONSIDERATIONS

The guilty suspect's statement is false; the others are true.

Assume that A is guilty. If so, A's statement is false. If so, this means that the other three must have made true statements. However, B says C is guilty; if A is guilty, A and B have both made false statements. Therefore, A is not guilty.

Assume that C is guilty. If so, B's statement, indicating that C is guilty, is true. However, if C is guilty, C's and D's statements are both false. Therefore, C is not guilty.

Assume that D is guilty. If so, B's statement indicating that C is guilty is false. Therefore, D is not guilty.

B is guilty. The other three make true statements:

A. T
B. F
C. T
D. T

SUMMARY SOLUTION B is the thief.

S3-2 The Forest Robber

CONSIDERATIONS
One suspect makes two true statements; one makes one true and one false statement; one makes two false statements.

Assume that A is guilty. If so, A's first and second statements are both false; B's first and second statements are both true; and C's first and second statements are both true. Therefore, A is not guilty

Assume that B is guilty. If so, each of the three suspects makes one true and one false statement. Therefore B is not guilty. Therefore, C is guilty.

	1	2
A	T	T
B	F	F
C	F	T

SUMMARY SOLUTION C is the robber.

S3-3 Two Pickpockets

CONSIDERATIONS
The two guilty ones each make only one true statement.

Assume that B is guilty. If so, B's first statement is true, as is either the second or third statement. Therefore, B is not one of the guilty ones. Assume that C is guilty. Since C's second statement indicates that B is not guilty, it is true. Also, if C is guilty, C's third statement must also be true. Therefore C is not guilty and the two guilty ones are A and D.

	1	2	3
A	F	F	T
B	F	F	T
C	F	T	F
D	T	F	F

SUMMARY SOLUTION A and D are the guilty ones.

S3-4 The Poacher

CONSIDERATIONS
Consider that the guilty suspect makes only one true statement.

Assume that A is guilty. If so, A's first statement indicating that D is innocent is true, as is his third statement, confirming that hunting is a source of food. Therefore, A is not guilty.

Assume that B is guilty. If so, B's second statement confirming that A is not the poacher is true, as is B's third statement indicating that his statements are not all true. Therefore B is not guilty.

Assume that D is guilty. D's first statement indicates that A's statements are not all true. If the statement is false, then A's first statement that D is innocent must be true. D's second statement, that at least one of C's statements is true, must itself be true if D is the poacher as claimed by C's second statement. Either D is innocent as confirmed by A's first statement, or else D has made two true statements. Therefore, D is not guilty. Therefore, C is guilty.

66

	1	2	3
A	T	T	T
B	F	T	T
C	F	F	T
D	F	T	T/F

SUMMARY SOLUTION C is the poacher.

S3-5 Property Destruction at the Village Inn

CONSIDERATIONS

The butcher's first statement is false, as all five were present. The baker's first statement agrees with the butcher's false first statement. Therefore, it also is false. The blacksmith's second statement is clearly false, from the description of the incident. The cobbler's first and third statements are contradictory. One is true and the other is false.

Therefore, the candlestick maker must be the one who makes no false statements. As indicated by his third statement, the baker did it.

	1	2	3	4
butcher	F	F	F	–
baker	F	T	F	–
candlestick maker	T	T	T	T
blacksmith	T	F	T	T
cobbler	F	F	T	F

SUMMARY SOLUTION The baker is guilty.

S3-6 Two Are Guilty

CONSIDERATIONS

Consider that one of the two culprits makes two true statements; the other makes two false statements.

Assume that A is guilty. If so, both statements are false. If so, B is also guilty. If so, B's statements must both be true. However, B's first statement claims innocence. Therefore, A is not guilty.

Assume that B is guilty. If so, since B claims innocence, both statements must be false. Therefore, if B is guilty, E's first statement must be true. However, since we know that at least A is innocent, E's first statement is false, as truthfully indicated by B. Therefore, B is not guilty.

Assume that E is guilty. If so, since we know E's first statement is false, both of his statements must be false. However, since we know that D's second statement is true, E's second statement is true. Therefore E is not guilty.

Therefore, the guilty ones are C, both of whose statements are false, and D, both of whose statements are true.

	1	2
A	T/F	T
B	T	T
C	F	F
D	T	T
E	F	T

SUMMARY SOLUTION C and D are the guilty ones.

S3-7 Pickpocket Thefts

CONSIDERATIONS

If either A or C is guilty, each of the four suspects makes two true statements.

Assume that A is guilty. If so, his first statement is false, since it was given that all four suspects were in town at the time of the last known theft. A's second statement would also be false. Therefore, A is not guilty.

Assume that C is guilty. If so, A's first and third statements are false, as are C's first and second statements. Therefore, C did not do it.

The guilty suspect must be B or D. Therefore, no two of the suspects make the same number of true statements. Therefore, one makes three true statements, one makes two true statements, one makes one true statement, and one makes no true statements.

Assume that B is guilty. If so, B's second and third statements are false and first statement is true; C's first and second statements are false and third statement is true. Therefore, B did not do it.

Therefore, D is guilty. C's statements are all false; A makes one true statement; D makes two true statements; and all three of B's statements are true.

	1	2	3
A	F	F	T
B	T	T	T
C	F	F	F
D	T	F	T

SUMMARY SOLUTION D is the pickpocket.

S3-8 D Is Missing

CONSIDERATIONS

Each suspect makes two true and one false statement. A's second statement and C's second statement are contradictory. One is true and one is false. Assume that C's second statement is false. If so, C's first and third statements must be true. If so, B's second statement is false, and first and third statements are true. This means that A's third statement and second statement are true, and first statement is false. However, if A's first statement is false, this contradicts B's first statement. Therefore, C's second statement is true.

A's second statement is false, and first and third statements are true. B's second statement is false, and first and third statements are true. C's second and third statements are true, and first statement is false. C is guilty.

	1	2	3
A	T	F	T
B	T	F	T
C	F	T	T

SUMMARY SOLUTION C is the burglar.

S3-9 The Unlucky Car Thief

CONSIDERATIONS

Consider that six statements are false. A's first statement and C's first statement contradict each other. One of them is false. C's third statement and D's second statement contradict each other. One of them is false. Therefore, there are four additional false statements.

Assume A is guilty. If so, A's second statement, B's second statement, and D's first statement are the additional false statements. This makes a total of five false statements. Therefore, A is not guilty.

Assume C is guilty. If so, A's second statement and D's first and third statements are false. This makes a total of five false statements. Therefore, C is not guilty.

Assume that D is guilty. If so, A's second statement, B's first statement, and D's third statement are false. Again, this makes a total of five false statements. Therefore, D did not do it.

Therefore, B is the culprit. B's third statement, C's second statement, and D's first and third statements are the additional false statements.

	1	2	3
A	T/F	T	T
B	T	T	F
C	F/T	F	T/F
D	F	F/T	F

SUMMARY SOLUTION B did it.

S3-10   The Oldest or the Youngest

CONSIDERATIONS
Each suspect makes only one true statement.

B's first statement and C's first statement are contradictory. One is true and one is false. B's second statement and C's third statement are contradictory. One is true and one is false. Since each makes only one true statement, B's third statement and C's second statement are both false. D is not the youngest, and C is not the oldest.

If A's first statement is true, the conclusion from A's second statement, which would be false, would be that B, the oldest, is guilty. From A's third statement, also false, we would conclude that C was also guilty. Therefore, A's first statement is false; B is not the oldest.

If D's second statement is true, B is guilty. However, from D's first statement, which would be false, we would conclude that the oldest was guilty. Since we know that B is not the oldest (A's false first statement), D's second statement is false. D's third statement is false, since it agrees with B's third statement, which we know to be false. Therefore D's first statement is true; the guilty one is the youngest.

Conclusions at this point are:

	1	2	3	oldest	youngest
A	F				
B			F	–	
C		F		–	
D	T	F	F		–

A's second statement agrees with D's first statement. Therefore, it is true, and A's third statement, that C is innocent, is false; C did it.

SUMMARY SOLUTION   C, the youngest, is guilty.

S4-1   Whose Group?

CONSIDERATIONS
Assume that A's first statement is true. If so, B's first statement is false and second statement must be true. If so, this means that C's second statement is true and first statement is false, which means that C is a Nororean. This contradicts A's second statement, which would be false. Therefore, A's first statement is false.

A is either a Midrorean or a Nororean. Assume A is a Midrorean, whose second statement is truthful. If so, B is a

Sororean, since the only other possibility would be Nororean, which would be inconsistent with B's true first statement. If so, B's second statement is also true. However, this is inconsistent with A's second statement. Therefore, A's second statement is false; A is a Nororean. Our conclusions, so far, are:

	Sororean	Nororean	Midrorean
A	–	+	–
B			
C			

C's first statement disagrees with A's second statement, which we know to be false. Therefore, C's first statement is true and, since C is not a Nororean (which A is), his second statement is false; C is a Midrorean.

Assume B's second statement is true. If so, B is a Midrorean, and his first statement is false. However, since A is a Nororean, for B's first statement to be false, B would have to be a Nororean. Therefore, B's second statement is false; B must be a Nororean, whose first statement is also false.

SUMMARY SOLUTION

A. Nororean
B. Nororean
C. Midrorean

S4-2   An Outlier

CONSIDERATIONS
Assume A's first statement, that he is the Outlier, is true. If so, A's second statement could be true or false. If A is the Outlier, B is the Sororean or the Midrorean. C, who claims

not to be the Outlier, must be the Sororean or the Midrorean. If so, D must be the Nororean. However, D's statement confirms C's statement. Therefore, A's first statement must be false, as is B's statement.

Since there is a Sororean, it must be C or D, and since C's first statement and D's statement agree, both are true. Therefore, A must be the Nororean. Since C's first statement is true, C is not the Outlier. If C were the Midrorean, his second statement would be false, making B the Midrorean. Therefore, C must be the Sororean. Thus, from C's second statement, B is not the Midrorean. Therefore, B is the Outlier, and D is the Midrorean.

	Sororean	Nororean	Midrorean	Outlier
A	–	+	–	–
B	–	–	–	+
C	+	–	–	–
D	–	–	+	–

SUMMARY SOLUTION

A. Nororean
B. Outlier
C. Sororean
D. Midrorean

S4-3   One of Each

CONSIDERATIONS

A's first statement claims that he is the Outlier. If true, A's third statement must be false. If so, B is not the Sororean. From B's third statement, if A is the Outlier, B must be the Midrorean, who has spoken falsely. (For a Nororean, the statement would be true, which is not possible.) If so, B's first statement must also be false. However, B's first statement asserts that A is the Outlier. Therefore, A is not the Outlier. B must be either the Outlier, whose first statement is false and third statement is truthful, or the Midrorean, whose first and third statements are false.

C's first and second statements and D's first statement are truthful. Therefore, A is the only one of the four who can be the Nororean and, if B is the Outlier, C must be the Sororean, and D is the Midrorean. If so, D's third statement must be truthful. However, it asserts that C's third statement is false. Therefore, B is not the Outlier; B is the Midrorean.

Our conclusions, so far, are:

	Sororean	Nororean	Midrorean	Outlier
A	–	+	–	–
B	–	–	+	–
C		–	–	
D		–	–	

From B's second statement, which truthfully claims C is not the Sororean, we can conclude that C, whose third statement is false, is the Outlier, and D is the Sororean.

SUMMARY SOLUTION

  A. Nororean
  B. Midrorean
  C. Outlier
  D. Sororean

S4-4 Olympic Games

CONSIDERATIONS

Assume that A was the winner of the one-half league run as indicated by his first statement. If so, his third statement must also be true. If so, A is a Sororean. However, A's second statement implies that C is a Sororean, while C's second statement indicates that A did not win the one-half league run, which is a contradiction. Therefore, A's first statement is false. Since A's third statement would be true for a Nororean, A must be either the Outlier or a Midrorean.

B's first statement and C's third statement are both truthful. However, B's third statement and C's first statement disagree; one is truthful and the other is false. Either B or C must be the Outlier. Therefore, A is a Midrorean, whose second statement must be truthful; C is a Sororean. Therefore, B is the Outlier.

	Sororean	Nororean	Midrorean	Outlier
A	−	−	+	−
B	−	−	−	+
C	+	−	−	−

SUMMARY SOLUTION

A. Midrorean
B. Outlier
C. Sororean

S4-5 One Is an Outlier

CONSIDERATIONS

Assume that B is the Outlier. If so, B's first statement is false. B's second statement must be false, since A's first statement must be true. B's third statement must be true (otherwise, B would be a Nororean). However, if not a Midrorean, C must be a Sororean, as the only other option would be for C to be a Nororean, and C's first statement would be true, not possible for a Nororean. C's second statement must be true. Therefore, B is not the Outlier. B's first and third statements must be true.

C could be a Sororean. However, C's third statement, claiming that D is a Sororean, must be false, as D's second statement is clearly false. C has made two consecutive true statements followed by a false statement. C is the Outlier.

At this point our conclusions are:

	Sororean	Nororean	Midrorean	Outlier
A				–
B				–
C	–	–	–	+
D				–

A, who has made three false statements, is a Nororean; B is a Sororean, and D is a Nororean, having made all false statements.

SUMMARY SOLUTION

A. Nororean
B. Sororean
C. Outlier
D. Nororean

S4-6 Olive Picking

CONSIDERATIONS

From A's second statement and B's first statement we can conclude that neither is the Sororean. If B's first statement is truthful, B is the Midrorean and, from B's third statement, C is the Outlier. However, if so, A must be the Nororean, and A's third statement, asserting that C is the Outlier, must be false. Therefore, B's first statement is false. If B's third statement were true, he'd be the Outlier, so the third statement must be false. Thus, B must be the Nororean.

The Sororean must be either C or D. Since C's second statement and D's first statement agree, both statements are true. Therefore, A's first statement is false. Therefore, A's second statement must be true; A is the Midrorean.

Since we know that B is the Nororean, with all false statements, D's third statement, agreeing with B's false second statement, is false. Therefore, since D's first statement is true and third statement is false, D is the Outlier. Therefore, C is the Sororean.

	Sororean	Nororean	Midrorean	Outlier
A	–	–	+	–
B	–	+	–	–
C	+	–	–	–
D	–	–	–	+

SUMMARY SOLUTION

A. Midrorean
B. Nororean
C. Sororean
D. Outlier

S4-7   Four for the Races

CONSIDERATIONS

Assume that A's third statement is truthful and C is the Outlier. If so, A's first statement is also truthful. If so, A is

78

either the Sororean or the Midrorean. If A is the Sororean, his second statement is truthful and D's first statement is false. If so, D's third statement should also be false. However, it affirms that A is the Sororean. Therefore, A is not the Sororean. If C is the Outlier and A is the Midrorean, A's second statement is false. If so, D's first statement is truthful and third statement is false. Therefore, C is not the Outlier.

A's third statement is false. Assume A is the Outlier; if so, his first statement must be truthful. If so, B's first statement is also truthful. However, B's second statement indicates that he is the Midrorean. If so, B's first statement is false, and if B's second statement is false, B is the Nororean. In either case, his first statement is false. Therefore, A is not the Outlier.

Therefore, A's first statement is false. If A is the Midrorean, his second statement is truthful. If so, D's first statement is false and D must be the Nororean. If so, B must be the Outlier, and C must be the Sororean. However, C's second statement confirms that B is the Midrorean. Therefore, B is not the Outlier, and A is not the Midrorean; A is the Nororean.

Our conclusions at this point are as follows:

	Sororean	Nororean	Midrorean	Outlier
A	−	+	−	−
B		−		−
C		−		−
D		−		

Therefore, the Outlier must be D. His third statement is false and first statement is truthful. B is the Midrorean as claimed by his truthful second statement, and C is the Sororean, with three truthful statements.

SUMMARY SOLUTION

A. Nororean
B. Midrorean
C. Sororean
D. Outlier

S4-8 Six Hyperboreans

CONSIDERATIONS

Philemon's first and third statements are contradictory, since Hesperus claims that Cadmus is the tax collector, the job also claimed by Philemon. Either Philemon's first statement or his third statement is false, or both of Philemon's statements are false, or Philemon is the Outlier.

Agenor's second and third statements are inconsistent, since he agrees that Hesperus's statements are all true, yet he claims that Cadmus is the chariot maker, although Hesperus's third statement indicates that Cadmus is the tax collector. At least one of Agenor's statements is false. It follows that Callisto's second statement, indicating that Agenor's statements are all true, is false.

Cadmus's first and fourth statements are inconsistent. Either or both are false, as he claims to be the olive grower, which agrees with Philemon's fourth statement, and also indicates that all of Philemon's statements are false.

Since Philemon, Agenor, Callisto and Cadmus have each made at least one false statement, the remaining candidates for the Sororean must be Alphenor and Hesperus.

Assume that Hesperus is the Sororean. This would mean that Alphenor is an Outlier, whose first statement is true, and second and third statements are false. It would also mean that Agenor is an Outlier, whose first and second statements are false and third statement is true. It would also mean that Philemon is an Outlier, whose first and fourth statements are false and third statement is true. Therefore, since there is only one Outlier, Hesperus is not the Sororean. Therefore, Alphenor is the Sororean. He is the tax collector, as claimed, and Hesperus is the chariot maker. Cadmus, who makes at least two consecutive true statements, his second and third, is the Outlier. Hesperus, whose first, third, and fourth statements are contradicted by Alphenor's second and third statements, is a Nororean. Agenor, whose second statement contradicts Alphenor's true third statement, and whose third statement agrees with Philemon's false third statement, is a Nororean. Callisto and Philemon are the two Midroreans. Callisto's first and third statements are true, and second statement is false. Philemon's second and fourth statements are true, and first and third statements are false. Cadmus's one false statement is his fourth one.

Our conclusions so far are:

	Sororean	Nororean	Midrorean	Outlier	Job
Agenor	−	+	−	−	
Alphenor	+	−	−	−	tax coll.
Cadmus	−	−	−	+	
Callisto	−	−	+	−	
Hesperus	−	+	−	−	chariot mkr.
Philemon	−	−	+	−	

Cadmus is the olive grower, as claimed. Callisto is the musician, as implied by her true first statement, as well as Philemon's true second statement. Since Hesperus falsely infers that Agenor is the wine maker, he must be the fishnet weaver, and Philemon is the wine maker.

SUMMARY SOLUTION

Agenor	Nororean	fishnet weaver
Alphenor	Sororean	tax collector
Cadmus	Outlier	olive grower
Callisto	Midrorean	musician
Hesperus	Nororean	chariot maker
Philemon	Midrorean	wine maker

S4-9 Chariot Race Winners

CONSIDERATIONS

Assume that Agathon's third statement is truthful. If so, Agathon's first statement is also true, unless he is the Outlier. Lysis's third statement contradicts Agathon's first statement. Therefore, if Agathon's third statement is truthful, then Lysis's third statement is truthful, and Agathon's first statement is false. Agathon could be the Outlier.

Lysis, however, claims that Phaedrus is a Sororean. Phaedrus's fourth statement, claiming that Protagoras is the Outlier, contradicts Lysis's first statement that Sosias is the Outlier. Therefore Lysis cannot be a Sororean. Therefore, Agathon's third statement is false and, unless he is the Outlier, his first statement is also false, and Lysis's third statement is true. Therefore, Lysis's first statement, claiming that Sosias is the Outlier, is also true, unless Lysis is the Outlier. Therefore, we can conclude that the Outlier is either Agathon, Lysis, or Sosias.

Phaedrus's fourth statement, claiming that Protagoras is the Outlier, is false. Therefore, Phaedrus's second statement, that Agathon is the Grand Champion, must also be false. Therefore, Lysis's fourth statement, that Agathon is not the Grand Champion, is true. Since we know that Lysis's second statement is false, Lysis is the Outlier. Therefore, Agathon's first and third statements are false. Therefore, Lysis is not the Grand Champion. Since we know that Phaedrus is not the Outlier, Agathon's fourth statement, agreeing with this, is true, as is his second statement, that Protagoras has had 15 wins. Agathon is a Midrorean. Also, we can conclude that Protagoras could not be the Grand Champion, since the Grand Champion would have to have had at least 18 wins. Protagoras's third statement, that Lysis is the Outlier, is true. His second statement that Sosias has had 15 wins is false, as we know that Protagoras has had fifteen wins, and no two racers have had the same number of wins. Therefore, Protagoras is a Midrorean, whose first and third statements are truthful and second and fourth statements are false. Agathon has had fewer wins than either Lysis or Protagoras.

Our conclusions, so far, are:

	Sororean	Nororean	Midrorean	Outlier	number of wins	Grand Champion
Agathon	+	−	+	−		−
Lysis	−	−	−	+		−
Phaedrus				−		
Protagoras	−	−	+	−	15	−
Sosias				−		

Sosias's second statement, asserting that Agathon has had more wins than Protagoras, is false, as is his third statement, claiming that Phaedrus is the Outlier. Therefore, Sosias is a Nororean, with all false statements. From Sosias's first statement, we can conclude that he has had six wins. Therefore, the Grand Champion is Phaedrus. From Sosias's fourth statement, we can conclude that Phaedrus's third statement, that Lysis has had the third-highest number of wins, is true. Therefore, Phaedrus's first statement is also true. Phaedrus, who has had 18 wins, is a Midrorean.

Since we know that Lysis has had the third-highest number of wins, that number must be 12, and Agathon, who has had fewer wins than Lysis, has had nine wins.

SUMMARY SOLUTION

Agathon	Midrorean	9 wins	
Lysis	Outlier	12 wins	
Phaedrus	Midrorean	18 wins	Grand Champion
Protagoras	Midrorean	15 wins	
Sosias	Nororean	6 wins	

S5-1 The Midville Muddlers

CONSIDERATIONS

From statement 6, Henry must be the center fielder. However, the indication that his batting average is lower than that of the catcher cannot be correct, considering statement 1. Statements 3 and 5 are also contradictory to statement 6. Therefore, statement 6 is false.

From statements 1 and 3, since Leo is not the catcher, he is the center fielder who bats .295. From statements 2 and 4, Leo must be one of the three players who are neighbors. Therefore Leo's surname is Clements. From statements 1 and 4, Ken, whose batting average is 30 points below Stan's, is the catcher, whose batting average is .280; Stan's batting average is .310. From statements 2 and 5, Stan's surname is Brooks, and he is the right fielder.

From statement 5, Henry's surname is not Ashley. Therefore, Henry is Dodson, the left fielder, whose batting average is .325. Ken's surname is Ashley.

first name	surname	position	batting avg.
Henry	Dodson	left field	.325
Ken	Ashley	catcher	.280
Leo	Clements	center field	.295
Stan	Brooks	right field	.310

SUMMARY SOLUTION

Henry Dodson	left fielder	.325
Ken Ashley	catcher	.280
Leo Clements	center fielder	.295
Stan Brooks	right fielder	.310

S5-2 Fishing Vacation Plans

CONSIDERATIONS

From statements 1, 3, 6, and 7, Barrott's first name is neither Andy, Bill, Carl, nor Dennis. Therefore, one of these four statements is the false one. From statement 5, Barrott was one of the two who are not married. This is contradictory to statement 3. Therefore, statement 3 is false.

Therefore, Barrott's first name is Carl. From statements 4 and 6, Dennis is not Whelan or Crowley. Therefore, Dennis is Cole.

From statements 4, 6, and 7, Whelan's favorite destination was the third, Crowley's was the last, and Barrott's was the first. Therefore, Cole's favorite destination was the second one.

Our conclusions so far are:

first name	surname	favorite location	order of trips
Andy			
Bill			
Carl	Barrott		1st
Dennis	Cole		2nd

From statement 4, the third destination was neither Patagonia nor New Zealand. Therefore, it was either Alaska or Iceland. From statement 6, the trip to New Zealand was not planned to be the first or the fourth destination. From statement 2, the trip to Iceland was planned for the year before the trip to Alaska. Therefore, the first trip must have been planned for Patagonia; the second trip, New Zealand; the third trip, Iceland; and the fourth trip, Alaska.

From statement 2, Andy's favorite destination was not Alaska (which, from statement 6, was Crowley's favorite). Therefore, Andy is Whelan and Bill is Crowley.

SUMMARY SOLUTION

Andy Whelan	Iceland	third
Bill Crowley	Alaska	fourth
Carl Barrott	Patagonia	first
Dennis Cole	New Zealand	second

S5-3 White-Water Rafting

CONSIDERATIONS

From statement 5, Henry and Hughes were on the same raft. However, this is inconsistent with statement 7, which states that Alan and Hughes were on the same raft. One of these two statements is false. Statement 7, which states that they were the first to finish, is inconsistent with statement 10, which indicates that they were last. Therefore, statement 7 is the false one.

From statement 6, Hawley was with Frank on the second-place yellow raft. From statements 2, 4, 6, and 10, Paul and Alan Wilson were on the third-place blue raft. From statement 1, Phil and Cook must be on the yellow raft, so they must be Phil Hawley and Frank Cook. From statements 2 and 5, Walt (who was not on the red raft) was on the green raft. From statements 2, 5, and 9, the partners on the red raft were Henry Gladstone and Don Hughes. From statements 3 and 8, the two on the green raft must have been LeRoy Sands and Walt Smith. O'Brien is Paul's surname.

SUMMARY SOLUTION

Alan Wilson / Paul O'Brien	blue raft	3rd place
Phil Hawley / Frank Cook	yellow raft	2nd place
Walt Smith / LeRoy Sands	green raft	1st place
Henry Gladstone / Don Hughes	red raft	did not finish

S5-4 Spelling Contest

CONSIDERATIONS

From statements 7 and 8, Jennings, who is one of the three young ladies, is not Lois or Helen. Therefore, Eleanor must be Jennings. However, this is inconsistent with statement 3. One of statements 3, 7, and 8 is false. Statement 5 is also inconsistent with statement 3. Therefore, statement 3 is false. Eleanor is Jennings.

From statements 6 and 7, Helen is not Knudson or Olsen, and from statement 1, she is not North. Therefore, Helen is Salisbury. From statement 4, Eric placed second. Therefore, from statement 6, he is not Knudson. From statement 4, Eric is not Olsen. Therefore, Eric is North. From statement 5, Gordie did not win, but placed higher than Jennings. Therefore, since Knudson placed fifth (statement 6), Gordie is Olsen and Lois is Knudson. Eleanor Jennings placed fourth, Gordie Olsen placed third, and Eric North placed second (statement 5). Helen Salisbury was the winner.

From statements 1 and 2, Lois misspelled "physiognomy," Eleanor misspelled "bivouac," Gordie misspelled "vicissitude," and Eric misspelled "isthmus."

SUMMARY SOLUTION

Eleanor Jennings	bivouac	4th place
Eric North	isthmus	2nd place
Gordie Olsen	vicissitude	3rd place
Helen Salisbury		1st place (winner)
Lois Knudson	physiognomy	5th place

CONSIDERATIONS

From statement 5, Curtis's spouse is an active Audubon member. From statement 3, Curtis's spouse is not Rosemary or Nancy. However, from statement 7, Nancy's husband is Curtis. Either statement 3, 5, or 7 is false. Statement 7 is also inconsistent with statement 10. Therefore, statement 7 is false. From statements 5 and 6, Angela is not married to Curtis. Therefore, Curtis's spouse is Susan (statements 3 and 5).

From statement 8, a pine siskin and a yellow warbler were sighted by the Dwyers. From statement 6, a lazuli bunting was sighted by Angela, and from statement 3, neither Rosemary nor Nancy is Dwyer. Therefore, Susan and Curtis are the Dwyers. From statement 10, Curtis was the last to sight his bird. Therefore, since the pine siskin was sighted early in the day (statement 8), it was sighted by Susan, and Curtis sighted the yellow warbler.

From statements 1 and 2, neither James nor William, who sighted a golden-crowned kinglet, is Brinkley. Therefore, Harold, who sighted a white-crowned sparrow (from statement 9), is Brinkley. From statement 3, neither Rosemary nor Nancy is Valentine. Therefore, Angela is Valentine. Since, from statement 1, James is not Valentine, William is Valentine and Angela's spouse. Therefore, James must be Eng. From statement 9, Nancy, who is not Harold Brinkley's spouse, must be the spouse of James Eng. Rosemary's spouse is Harold.

From statements 4 and 9, Nancy was not the first to sight a western tanager or a black-headed grosbeak. Therefore, she was first to sight an acorn woodpecker. Since, from statement 1, James was not the first to sight a western tanager, he was the first to sight a black-headed grosbeak. Rosemary was the first to spot a western tanager.

SUMMARY SOLUTION

Angela Valentine	lazuli bunting
William Valentine	golden-crowned kinglet
Curtis Dwyer	yellow warbler
Susan Dwyer	pine siskin
Harold Brinkley	white-crowned sparrow
Rosemary Brinkley	western tanager
James Eng	black-headed grosbeak
Nancy Eng	acorn woodpecker

S5-6 Car Pool

CONSIDERATIONS

From statement 1, Amarol must be one of the three women. This, however, is inconsistent with statement 7. Also, from statement 1, Amarol is the first to be dropped off in the evening. This is inconsistent with both statements 3 and 6. Therefore, statement 1 is false.

From statement 2, neither Neal nor Florence is the secretary. From statements 3 and 4, since the secretary is the second to be picked up in the morning, Paul, who is the sixth to be picked up in the morning, is not the secretary. From statement 6, since Gloria is dropped off immediately after Avenal, who is dropped off first (statement 3), she is dropped off second, and Evelyn, who is dropped off two people later, is the fourth to be dropped off in the evening. Since the secretary is the fifth to be dropped off in the evening (statement 4), neither Gloria nor Evelyn is the secretary. Therefore, Milton, the secretary, is the second to be picked up in the morning and the fifth to be dropped off in the evening.

From statement 7, Avenal and Amarol are two of the three men. Since Paul is not Avenal (statement 3), and, from statement 6, Amarol is the third to be dropped off (immediately before Evelyn, who is the fourth to be dropped off), Milton is not Amarol. Therefore, Paul is Amarol, and Neal is Avenal, the first to be dropped off. Therefore, Florence is Adams the attorney, who is the first to be picked up in the morning and the sixth to be dropped off in the evening (statement 5). From statement 6, Gloria, who is picked up immediately after Neal and before Paul, is the fifth to be picked up, and Neal is the fourth to be picked up in the morning. Therefore, Evelyn is the 3rd to be picked up in the morning.

From statement 2, the secretary (who is Milton) is neither Agassi nor Atwater. Therefore, Milton is Altchech. From statement 4, Paul Amarol, who is the third to be dropped off in the evening, is the word processing supervisor. From statement 8, the personnel manager, who is not the fourth or fifth to be picked up in the morning, is Evelyn; since she is not Atwater, she is Agassi, and Gloria is Atwater. From statement 7, since Neal Avenal is not the systems analyst, he is the computer programmer, and Gloria Atwater is the systems analyst.

SUMMARY SOLUTION

carpoolers	positions	a.m. pickup	p.m. drop-off
Evelyn Agassi	personnel manager	3rd	4th
Florence Adams	attorney	1st	6th
Gloria Atwater	systems analyst	5th	2nd
Milton Altchech	secretary	2nd	5th
Neal Avenal	computer programmer	4th	1st
Paul Amarol	word processing supervisor	6th	3rd

S5-7 Summer Students

CONSIDERATIONS

From statement 5, Professors Harrison and White teach in buildings at the two ends of the row. This is contradictory to statement 8, which is also contradictory to statement 7. Therefore, statement 8 is false.

From statements 4, 5, 6, and 7, Professors Harrison and White teach in buildings A and F, not necessarily in that order. Professor Landers teaches in building B. Professor Carson does not teach in building D. Therefore, he teaches in building C or E, and Professor Denton, whose building is not adjacent to that of Professor Carson, must also teach in C or E. Therefore, Professor Bradford's building is D.

From statements 4, 5, 6, and 7, Professor Denton does not teach music; neither Professor Harrison nor Professor White teach music or psychology; Professor Landers does not teach music, and Professor Carson teaches law. Therefore Professor Bradford teaches music in building D with Sawyer as his student (statement 11). From statement 2, Carl, who is not attending class in buildings A or F (he is between Sawyer and Burt), is studying history. Therefore, Professors Harrison and White teach economics and English, not necessarily in that order.

From statement 10, John's class is in the building next to Professor Harrison's building. Therefore, John's building is either B or E. Since Rogers, who is not John, attends class in building B (Professor Landers's building), John's building is E. Therefore, Professor Harrison's building is F, and Professor White's building is A.

From statement 2, Carl, whose class is in the building between those of Sawyer and Burt, is studying history (statement 2) from Professor Denton in building C. Therefore, John is studying law under Professor Carson in building E. Burt Rogers is studying psychology (the remaining subject) under Professor Landers in building B.

Conclusions at this point are:

first name	surname	subject	professor	building
Burt	Rogers	psychology	Landers	B
Carl		history	Denton	C
Fran				
John		law	Carson	E
Louise				
Victoria				

professor	subject	building
Bradford	music	D
Carson	law	E
Denton	history	C
Harrison		F
Landers	psychology	B
White		A

From statement 9, Fran's building is not A or F (nor is Williams's). Therefore, her surname is Sawyer. She is studying music under Professor Bradford in building D. From statement 1, Louise, whose class is in building A, must be studying economics from Professor White. Victoria is studying English under Professor Harrison in building F. From statement 3, since Peterson's building is adjacent to Victoria's, John is Peterson, Carl is Williams (statement 9), Louise is West (statement 1), and Victoria is Karr.

first name	surname	subject	professor	building
Burt	Rogers	psychology	Landers	B
Carl	Williams	history	Denton	C
Fran	Sawyer	music	Bradford	D
John	Peterson	law	Carson	E
Louise	West	economics	White	A
Victoria	Karr	English	Harrison	F

S5-8   Chess Players

CONSIDERATIONS

Of the six members of the City Chess Club, Edith is the only female. From statement 9, she usually opens with the Stonewall System. However, from statement 6, Edith always opens with a king's pawn; the Stonewall System is a queen's pawn opening. One of statements 6 and 9 is false. However, from statement 2, Draper, who is a male, prefers the Stonewall System, and since no two players prefer the same opening, statement 9 is the false one.

From statements 3, 4, and 7, the two strongest players are Harry Duvall and Fred Evans. From statements 1 and 5, George's surname is not Gruber or Campbell. Therefore, George is either Davis or Draper. Besides George, the other possibilities for Draper are Dan and Jeff. From statement 5, Campbell is not Edith or Jeff. Therefore, Dan's surname is Campbell. Since, from statement 5, Jeff prefers to open with the Ruy Lopez, and, from statement 2, Draper prefers the Stonewall System, George's surname is Draper.

From statement 5, Dan Campbell favors the King's Gambit opening. Since Jeff prefers the Ruy Lopez, from statement 6, Edith prefers the third king's pawn opening, the Bishop's opening. From statement 4, Edith prefers the

Pirc Defense against king's pawn openings and the Meran Defense against queen's pawn openings. Therefore, Edith is Gruber and Jeff is Davis (statements 1, 3, and 4). From statement 2, Draper prefers to open with the Stonewall System. From statement 7, Evans does not favor the Queen's Gambit opening. Therefore, he prefers the Colle System and Harry prefers the Queen's Gambit opening. Our conclusions so far are:

first name	surname	preferred opening move	preferred king's pawn defense	preferred queen's pawn defense
Dan	Campbell	King's Gambit		
Edith	Gruber	Bishop's	Pirc	Meran
Fred	Evans	Colle System		
George	Draper	Stonewall System		
Harry	Duvall	Queen's Gambit		
Jeff	Davis	Ruy Lopez		

From statement 1, Jeff Davis must be the player who prefers the Sicilian Defense against king's pawn openings and the Tarrasch Defense against queen's pawn openings. From statement 10, Dan Campbell prefers the King's Indian Defense against queen's pawn openings. From statements 3 and 8, Fred Evans does not favor the French Defense, the Caro-Kann Defense, or Petroff's Defense against king's pawn openings. Therefore, he prefers the Two Knights Defense. From statements 7 and 10, Fred prefers the Benoni Defense against queen's pawn openings. From statement 2, Draper uses the Nimzo-Indian Defense against queen's pawn openings, and Harry Duvall uses the remaining defense against queen's pawn openings, the Cambridge Springs Defense.

From statements 2 and 3, Dan Campbell uses the French Defense against king's pawn openings, and Harry Duvall favors Petroff's Defense. The remaining defense against king's pawn openings, the Caro-Kann Defense, is preferred by George Draper.

SUMMARY SOLUTION

full name	preferred opening move	preferred king's pawn defense	preferred queen's pawn defense
Dan Campbell	King's Gambit	French Defense	King's Indian Defense
Edith Gruber	Bishop's Opening	Pirc Defense	Meran Defense
Fred Evans	Colle System	Two Knights Defense	Benoni Defense
George Draper	Stonewall System	Caro-Kann Defense	Nimzo-Indian Defense
Harry Duvall	Queen's Gambit	Petroff's Defense	Cambridge Springs Defense
Jeff Davis	Ruy Lopez	Sicilian Defense	Tarrasch Defense

Index

Page key: puzzle, *hints*, **solution**